Forgive and Let Go!
A book about forgiveness

Cheri J. Meiners

★

illustrated by Elizabeth Allen

free spirit
PUBLISHING®

Library of Congress Cataloging-in-Publication Data
Meiners, Cheri J., 1957–
     Forgive and let go! : a book about forgiveness / by Cheri J. Meiners ; Illustrated by Elizabeth Allen.
          pages cm. — (Being the best me! series)
     ISBN 978-1-57542-485-9 (hard cover) — ISBN 1-57542-485-1 (hard cover) — ISBN 978-1-57542-487-3 (pbk.) — ISBN 1-57542-487-8 (pbk.)
1. Forgiveness—Juvenile literature. I. Allen, Elizabeth (Artist) illustrator. II. Title.
     BJ1476.M45 2015
     179'.9—dc23
                                                                                   2014035346

Free Spirit Publishing does not have control over or assume responsibility for author or third-party websites and their content.

Reading Level Grade 1; Interest Level Ages 4–8;
Fountas & Pinnell Guided Reading Level I

Cover and interior design by Tasha Kenyon and Janet LaMere
Edited by Alison Behnke

10 9 8 7 6 5 4 3 2 1
Printed in Hong Kong
P17200215

Free Spirit Publishing Inc.
Minneapolis, MN
(612) 338-2068
help4kids@freespirit.com
www.freespirit.com

To my brothers
Victor, Robert, and Erik:
For letting go of differences
and holding on to each other
through thick and thin.

I like to get along with people.

When something goes wrong
or annoys me,

2

I might not be able to stop it, or change it.
But I can decide to let it go.

Sometimes people make mistakes
or do things that bother me.

If a problem isn't that important, I might choose to forget about it.

5

I might feel hurt, frustrated, or angry.

I can take a few deep breaths.

I'll try to cool down
and think about what to do.

When I feel offended, it may help to talk to the person.

I can also listen to how that person feels.

If someone says, "I'm sorry"
and tries to make things right,

I'm sorry.

People are usually trying
hard to do their best.

I can let mistakes go
and give someone
another chance.

I make mistakes, too.
If I argue and try to show that I'm right,
I'm probably not listening.

I can say, "I'm sorry." I want to be kind more than I want to always be right.

I'm sorry. You can use it first.

18

Sometimes a person doesn't apologize.
I can still decide to forgive.

It might help me if I imagine
the person saying, "I'm sorry."

21

Things don't always seem fair.
But if I don't let go of what bothers me,
I might miss out on good things
around me.

I know people who care about me.

They can listen
and be there to help me
if I feel that someone
has let me down.

I want to choose kind thoughts
and always look for the good in others.

I can let go of feeling hurt, and think of ways to get along.

I might do something nice
to show that I'm really over it.

When I forgive, it's good for that person,
and I feel better, too.

Forgiveness doesn't change what happened, but it can change me.

I want to be kind and let mistakes go.
I want to be my very best.

Ways to Reinforce the Ideas in *Forgive and Let Go!*

Forgive and Let Go! focuses on forgiveness—the ability to let go of anger and resentment when we feel wronged. Forgiveness skills include being willing to accept apologies and offer them, working to rebuild and strengthen relationships when conflicts arise, and adopting thoughts and behaviors that help us recover from hurt feelings. Forgiveness is a choice—an act of strength that counteracts feelings of helplessness and sadness. It can lead to improved physical and mental health, a sense of healing, deeper feelings of fulfillment and relief from stress, improved relationships, and a greater sense of control over one's life—all of which can lead to greater happiness. Young children can begin to develop forgiveness skills and grow in their ability to forgive and let go as they incorporate principles discussed in this book. In addition, the activities on pages 33–35 can help children develop the qualities of understanding, respect, and patience that accompany true forgiveness. Here is a quick summary of eight forgiveness skills, most of which are mentioned in the children's text:

1. Ignore little things that bother you.

2. Cool down when you feel upset.

3. Talk and listen to others to resolve misunderstandings.

4. Accept other people's apologies.

5. Imagine that a person has apologized to you.

6. Apologize for things you've done that may have hurt someone else.

7. Choose positive and kind thoughts to replace negative feelings.

8. Show kindness and forgiveness by doing something nice for a person you have disagreed with.

Words to know:
Here are terms you may want to discuss.

accept: to understand when something can't be changed

annoy: to bother or irritate

apologize: to say "I'm sorry" for doing something that hurt another person

argue: to give or tell reasons against something

blaming: saying or feeling that something is someone else's fault

forgive: to stop being angry with someone

let go: to move past something that bothered you

offended: insulted or hurt

As you read each spread, ask children:
- What is happening in this picture?

- What is the main idea?

- How would you feel if you were this person?

Here are additional questions you might discuss:
Pages 1–7
- How does getting along with people make you feel happy?

- What is something you do to treat people well?

- What is a little thing that annoys you?

- What does it mean to "let it go"? Why do you think it's a good idea to let little things go?

- Think about a time that someone did something you didn't like. How did you feel about it? What is a new way you could think about the situation and let it go?

Pages 8–15
- Take a big, deep breath. How can a deep breath help you cool down? What are some other ways to cool down? *(Examples: Count to ten, take a walk, sing a favorite song.)*

- Why is it a good idea to stop and think about what to do?

- What can you learn by listening to another person when you disagree? Why do you think listening is better than arguing?

- If a person doesn't say "I'm sorry," do you think you should still forgive the person? Why or why not?

- Imagine that someone is saying "I'm sorry" to you after a disagreement. How does it feel to think about this imaginary apology? Do you feel any different? *(Research shows that imagining an apology can produce feelings of calmness and resolution even if no apology takes place. This strategy can help children move past hurt feelings and disagreements.)*

- Think of a time you thought something wasn't fair. How did that feel for you? How do you think you would feel if you could let it go?

- Name a person who cares about you. What do you think that person will do if you ask for help?

- How can it help you let go of other people's mistakes if you remember that you make mistakes, too?

- Why is it hard to really listen to someone if you are arguing or blaming?

- Do you think it's important to always be right? Why or why not? When you think you are right and someone else is wrong about something, how do you feel? What can you do at those times? *(You may wish to discuss how getting along, developing relationships, and being kind to people can bring us more satisfaction than always having the "right" answer. There are also times when people just have different ideas, and there is no single right point of view. Being kind and respectful can help everyone feel better about the situation.)*

- Do you think that apologizing is a good idea even when another person has also been hurtful? Why or why not?

- How do you feel when you choose to find the good in other people? How can this help you forgive?

- How can forgiveness be good for the other person? Why is it good for you?

- How do you think forgiving someone else can change you?

- How does forgiving someone help you be your best?

- What is something you will try to let go of? What can you think about to help you let go?

Games and Activities for Forgiving and Letting Go

Read this book often with your child or group of children. Once children are familiar with the book, refer to it when teachable moments arise—both those involving healthy and positive letting go of hurt feelings and those relating to anger, frustration, and resentment. In addition, use the following activities to reinforce children's understanding of forgiving and letting go.

A Taste of Letting Go

(Be sure to check with parents and caregivers about food allergies before doing this activity.)

Materials: Lemon juice, horseradish, or other foods with a bitter or sour taste; honey, small candies, or other sweet foods; small spoons (1 or 2 for each child)

Directions: Let children taste a small amount of something bitter or sour. Talk about how that taste could be similar to the emotions they may feel when they are angry at or hurt by someone. Then let the children taste something sweet. The sweet taste replaces the bitter one. Talk about how we can work to replace our hurt and angry thoughts with happier, forgiving thoughts. These thoughts can help us feel better and get along with others.

Shake Hands and Shake It Off

Directions: Put on some fun background music if you choose. You will be the "caller" as in a square dance. First, children line up in two parallel lines facing each other. When you call "Shake hands," children shake hands with the people across from them in the opposite line. (Take time to teach a nice, firm handshake while looking and smiling at the person.)

As children shake hands, one person says, "I'm sorry." The other replies, "I forgive you." Then have each child say the opposite phrase. Next, call "Shake it off." Children can move around in their spots as if shaking off hurt feelings—dusting off their shoulders, or just wiggling. Then call "Move on." At that point, children in one line stay put while children in the opposite line move to their right and stand in front of the next person across from them. (The first person in the moving line goes to the other end of the line.) When you call "Shake hands" again, they can shake the next person's hand. Continue, periodically calling "Shake hands," "Shake it off," and "Move on" until children reach their original partners.

Let It Go

Materials: Small pieces of paper; pencils or crayons; recycling bin

Directions: Pass out paper and help each child privately write or draw about a time when he or she felt wronged. Then help children fold their papers into airplanes, and release them by gliding them into a recycling bin set a few feet away.

Discussion: Discuss with children how they can let go of hurt feelings, grudges, or bad memories like they let go of their paper airplanes. Even though they may remember what happened, they can decide to let go of the negative feelings and feel happier. Tell children to "take a picture" of the airplane in their mind, so they can remind themselves to let go of problems. (You may wish to review the eight forgiveness skills summarized on page 32 or in the story, and discuss how each strategy can help them let go of negative emotions.)

Holding Heavy Grudges

Materials: Index cards; clean pebbles or small rocks; plastic ziplock bags; doll or character toy (for Variation)

Directions: Write scenarios on individual index cards. You can use the sample scenarios at the end of the activity or create your own. Seat children on the floor around the pile of pebbles. Read a scenario card. Have children think of a time that something similar has happened to them. Then have children who

relate to the scenario pick up a rock and place it in a ziplock bag on their lap. Explain that holding the rocks is like holding grudges, and talk about how it feels. Continue to read scenarios, allowing children to gather rocks. Have children carry a rock in their hand, or put a plastic bag of pebbles in a pocket for the next hour or so as they go about other activities. Meet again, and ask children how it felt to carry the rocks, and how it compares to holding grudges. Talk about how we can let go of grudges and hurt feelings if we choose; allow children to put their rocks back.

Variation: Help a child draw and read a scenario card. Then discuss how a person might feel in this situation. Have the child pretend that the doll or character toy is the person who hurt him or her. After talking to the doll and practicing forgiving, the child can put a rock back on the pile. (If children need guidance, you can use the Forgiveness Phrases on page 35 as prompts.)

Scenarios

- Someone is playing with Sam's toy and breaks it.
- Someone draws on Josefina's picture.
- Someone won't let Alexei play with him or her.
- Someone blames Dominique for a thing she didn't do.
- Someone bumps, pushes, or hits Wally.
- Someone lies to Sophie.
- Someone calls Isaac a mean name or says something else that hurts his feelings.
- Someone won't share with Mara.

Let It Go—Don't Blow Your Top!

Materials: 2 1-quart glass jars (such as canning jars); marker that writes on glass; ½ cup white vinegar; ½ cup water; 2 tablespoons baking soda

Preparation: Using the marker, draw the simple face of a child on each jar. Put the vinegar in one jar and the water in the other. At the appropriate times in the discussion, add 1 tablespoon of baking powder to each jar. The jar with the vinegar will bubble up.

Discussion: Talk about two children, represented by the two jars. One child (the jar with water) tries to forgive people and let go of disagreements. The other child (the jar with vinegar) looks a lot like the first child on the outside. But inside, this child is feeling angry and has a hard time letting go of hurt feelings. One day, the same thing happens to both children. For example, someone calls each child a name or won't let them join in playing a game. Ask children to predict how the first child will react. Add the baking soda to the jar with water. Discuss how this child was upset at first, but calms down and lets it go. Then have children predict how the second child will react. Add the baking soda and observe the chemical reaction. Ask questions like, "Why do you think the children reacted differently to the same thing?" "Which child was happier?" and "What happens when we don't let go of our hurt feelings?"

Letting Go: Feelings That Weigh Me Down

Materials: A backpack; a dozen or so small- or medium-sized cans of food; plain white paper; scissors; tape or glue; pen or marker; index cards; recycling bin; action figures or dolls (for Level 2)

Preparation: Cover the can labels with paper. Write a Weighed Down scenario on each can, using those listed in the next column or your own ideas. Also write one Forgiveness Phrase (next column) on each of 8 index cards. Put several cans of food in the backpack.

Level 1

Let each child try on the backpack to see how heavy it is. Have the child pull a can out of the backpack. Read the label on the can aloud (or help the child read it). Ask children, "In this situation, what could the child say or do to show that he or she forgives and lets go?" As a prompt, a child may draw a Forgiveness Phrase card and give that response. Then a child may "let go" by putting the can in the recycling bin. (It can be retrieved after the game.) Continue in the same way until all the cans are gone. Let children try on the empty pack; compare it to people's feelings when they let go of negative emotions.

Level 2

Role-play each situation with action figures or dolls. Then let children role-play the scene themselves and demonstrate how they could forgive.

Variation: As a review, the activity can be played without props. Make a set of Weighed Down cards to go with the Forgiveness Phrase cards by writing each scenario on an index card. Have children draw a card and talk about or role-play how they could resolve the problem and let it go.

Weighed Down Sample Scenarios

- Elise keeps thinking about an argument she had with a friend.
- Nicolas feels annoyed that someone won't play with him.
- Serena feels angry and wants to get even with someone.
- Erik said "I hate you" to someone.
- Asmahan is remembering mean things that someone said to her.
- Emmanuel's feelings are hurt because of something someone did by mistake.
- Cammi is not being patient when someone takes a long time to do something.
- Hugo is blaming someone for breaking something.

Forgiveness Phrases

1. "I forgive you. Will you forgive me?"
2. "I'm not mad anymore."
3. "Don't worry about it."
4. "I make mistakes, too."
5. "I'm sorry I was angry with you."
6. "Let's be friends again."
7. "I let it go."
8. "It's okay now."

Get the Whole
Being the Best Me! Series
by Cheri J. Meiners

Books that help young children develop character traits and attitudes that strengthen self-confidence, resilience, decision-making, and a sense of purpose.
Each book: 40 pp., color illust., HC and PB, 11¼" x 9¼", ages 4–8.

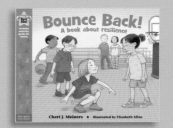

Learning to Get Along® Series Interactive Software

Free Spirit's
Learning to Get Along®
Series by Cheri J. Meiners

Help children learn, understand, and practice basic social and emotional skills. Real-life situations, diversity, and concrete examples make these read-aloud books appropriate for childcare settings, schools, and the home.
Each book: 40 pp., color illust., PB, 9" x 9", ages 4–8.

www.freespirit.com • 800.735.7323
Volume discounts: edsales@freespirit.com • Speakers bureau: speakers@freespirit.com